SWEET
Emotions

SWEET
Emotions

Illustrated By Stephen Cole
Secret ingredients... In life walk in true faith &
In your recipes mix with true love.
Then you're sure to be filled with favor & flavor.
The F & F of Life.

KEVIN BATES

LitPrime
"Your story is our priority"

LitPrime Solutions
21250 Hawthorne Blvd
Suite 500, Torrance, CA 90503
www.litprime.com
Phone: 1-800-981-9893

Published by LitPrime Solutions   01/17/2023

ISBN: 979-8-88703-109-5(sc)
ISBN: 979-8-88703-110-1(e)

Library of Congress Control Number: 2022922742

Contents

Section 1
(First Course or Appetizers)

Section 2
Salad

Section 3
(Main Course or Entrée)

Section 4
(Chef's Special)

Section 5
(Beverages)

Section 6
(Desserts)

Thanks & Dedications

First I would like to give thanks to God who has given me all I've asked for & more in life. He has sent me the 'Gifts of Life.' 'The Savior & family. Jesus who came & died for our sins & the strong bond of family love to make me stronger in my faith. Thank my mother & the strong black ladies before her who house who we look forward to going to on a Sunday afternoon after church to eating a Sunday dinner.

A shout out to great teachers of words and mind...Apostle David Roberson working with Pastor Wanda Roberson. Poets of the past Langston Hughes & Maya Angelo. Poets & teacher Nikki Giovanni & Gil Scott Heron always motivate the mind when I hear you speak. Thank everyone for helping the mind & body grow.

I dedicate this book to two of my nephews & their love for food. First my brother's third son Jamel Bates who @ 21 from his love of food has a food business where he prepares great meals that people are in demand for. My sister's only son @ 18 who has a great passion for food makes unbelievable meals for the family & has written his own cookbook. Shoutout to past cooks in the family Selena Green & Eric Avrey.

Last & upmost thanks the two greatest sounding board in my life my mother Mary Bates & the Illustrator of drawings Stephen Cole great inspirations in creating this book.

Book Synopsis

Sweet Emotions is a book created by me off the emotions that my mother's cooking & love for cooking & sharing it with others would bring. I hope everything within the covers of this book to bring those sweet emotions. When you would enjoy a great meal you get an unbelievable rush & can't wait for the next plate. That is what my mother's food brought & I hope my word to do the same to have you wanting the next poem to have the feeling of 'Sweet Emotions' when you read my words. Then the same after you cook each recipe. The book takes you from your appetizers to your desserts.

Sweet Emotions

Section 1

(First Course or Appetizers)

Ahh!

There has been rejection in my life,
yet I have to take it all in stride,
love of my past was not meant to be.

When they left I even made one last plea.
You appeared like an angel of lost love,
I eagerly welcome you in my heart.

Would the day come you'd be my wife?
You said I love you I got misty eyed,
at that moment I got on bended knee.

An addition to our life baby makes three,
just as precious and peaceful as a white dove.
My love for you two is grand it's off the chart.

Rewards for you being in my life makes me say "Ahh!"

Breath Of Life

Breath of life seems to leave his soul.
Love of false glamour fills his mind.
Unknown tomorrow clouds his goal;
Suffocation of the word from his greed.
He prays for forgiveness so he'll be whole.

We have faith then we can breathe again.
Installed is a seed waiting to open up.
Now prayer is up and favor is raining;
Everything changes and there is great gain.

Brighter Tomorrow

You'd brag about evil plans
produce by your pride.
Creating an uncertainty in life

Love, joy, and compassion
gives a brighter tomorrow
burns the mist of yesterday.

Embrace everyone with
loving blessed heart.
Embody the Lords word.

Walk your life in faith
He will reach out...Showing
a door to His world.

Domination

Boldly she will walk into any room;
Lovely is her presence of beauty.
Ultimate dominance she's a boom!
She gathers attention from everyone
Her day of glory is not to be assume

We honor the God given black queen
In our lives we have a gift from above
None more power as she struts along
Even bigger than the stars on the screen.

Good

Brought together by a rhythmic dance.
Longing to share a dinner with you,
Unknown if I'll be allowed this chance.
Special is your given name; one of queens.
Hoping to be the king of your romance.

Wonder who told me you were so good?
It's in your sweet voice with that joyous laugh.
Never hoping that I'm misunderstood.
Elation would be to hold your soft hand.

Lady Cornhusker

Oh my sweet Lady Cornhusker
with such a varied personality
colorful attracting many to her.

Rich in characteristics able to
attribute to the needs of many.
Beneath her appealing beauty
there lies an engaging nature.

Sweet Lady Cornhusker

Roasted Corn Salsa

Ingredients:
2 Ears of corn, 1Red bell pepper, 2 Garlic
cloves peeled, minced, 1 Chipotle Chile, dice,
1 tablespoon fresh cilantro, chopped,
Salt & Black Pepper to taste

Prepare an outdoor or indoor grill. Shuck corn &
remove silk. Grill corn until each side is golden brown.
Let cool. Roost red pepper on the grill until charred on
all sides. Place pepper in a towel or covered container
to let steam. Remove when cool. Peel charred skin off
the pepper, remove stem and seeds & dice the flesh.

Cut kernels from the corncobs. In a medium mixing
bowl combine corn, roasted bell peppers, garlic, Chile
& cilantro. Season with salt & black pepper. Serve with
tortilla chips or as a topping for tacos. Makes 3 cups.
Chef's notes: marinate corn after shucking along with
peppers for 8 hours before grilling for better flavor.

Section 2

Salad

A Picnic of Love

We take a ride to the countryside in a blue convertible,
Top down enjoying the sunshine and wind blowing,
In the back seat lies a checkered blanket and cooler,
Mostly we have God's blessing, each other and our love.

We arrive to a beautiful secluded spot filled with flowers,
The colors and aromas over take us
as we lay out the blanket,
Jazz music plays as the birds sing our sweetest love song.
While we arrange a feast fit for two true love birds.

Under a giant Oak Tree we sip on Mango Iced Tea,
No need for wine intoxicated on our empowering love.
We dine on Black-Eyed Pea salad and
Honey Glaze Fried Chicken,
My eyes that will never leave you while
I yearn for your sweet lips.

Carving our names into that Oak we
profess our love be as strong.
Sitting at the stream nearby we let
the water run over our feet,
Throwing pebbles declaring each one
and ripple signifies our years.
This one gorgeous excursion turns into...

A Picnic of Love

Black-Eyed Pea Salad
Texas Caviar

Ingredients: Two 15-ounce cans black-eyed peas, drained and rinsed
1/4 red onion, finely chopped
1/4 cup roughly chopped fresh parsley
1/4 cup red wine vinegar
2 tablespoons extra-virgin olive oil
3 cloves garlic, minced
1 can of Rotel chopped tomatoes hot
Dash hot sauce, such as Tabasco
Kosher salt and freshly ground black pepper
Kosher salt and freshly ground black pepper

Combine the black-eyed peas, red onions, parsley, vinegar, oil, garlic, can of Rotel tomatoes and hot sauce in a bowl. Season with salt and pepper. Cover with plastic wrap and refrigerate at least 3 hours and up to 24 hours. Serve with tortilla chips.

Black Rose

Black Rose teachings opens many minds
Leader lowly at heart build our future.
Understand her words we're to incline.
Such a beautiful soul of the Lord above.
Her duties on earth being done as assigned.

We're thankful the Black Rose come our way;
In our hearts we carry much love for her.
None like this teacher of life and much else.
Everyone stands, cheers and say Happy Birthday!

Butterfly Effect

I was wandering from place to place
then I came into a small synagogue.
Apostle asks, "what are you looking for?"
My reply was "I do not know I am lost."

Told me in time I was to be empowered,
Prophecy told me I would prosper.
I begin to walk in true faith trust the Lord,
the small seed inside begin to grow.

I was driven to serve to Lord above
a pleasure to hear his teachings
fed off his word like a caterpillar to a leaf.
Transformation had begun belief in the word.

Jesus indeed has the ability to change us,
we will see things in a different light.
Believe in Him and ourselves
you will become who God created.

Countryside

I went to a place long forgotten by the one I love,
On a cool fall day in broken down blue convertible,
Engine worn down top ragged blowing in the wind,
I arrive at an abandoned countryside area.

A dead Oak whose leaves have fallen like my tears,
Out stretched limbs as my arms the reach for my love.
A few birds now that only sing songs of sorrow,
No flowers of beauty with their aroma to give hope.

The stream has dried up but my love for you has not.
I look to the skies ask the Lord for a sign if meant to
be, Then comes a sudden rain filling that stream once
again, Washing away what grief I came here with.

Knowing love come not from a physical nature,
Not even our surroundings make up our love.
It's about giving one one's self and dedication.
Reminded to always look within a trip to this...

Countryside

Heavenly Rose

Brought to us by God this Heavenly Rose.
Lovely at birth shouted joy and thanked God!
Unfortunately Heavenly Rose was called back home
She's respected and loved and remain in our hearts
No parent wants to say goodbye to their child.

At least the Nettles know their Rose goes home.
In Christ we pray and bless the lovely family.
There's a dark evening yet there's light tomorrow
Favor will come in God's time stay on His path.

Hunger

There is a great desire for you.
The sweet fragrance of love
fills the air around us both.
Perfume of your flesh is aromatic.

A great hunger to go into
your valley of rose petals.
Fly with the birds and bees,
taste the honey of your hips.

Men's Fav Green Cabbage Salad

Ingredients: 1(2 ½ lb) Green cabbage, outer leaves dis carded,   1 medium onion, halved lengthwise, then thinly sliced crosswise 2 tablespoons chopped fresh flat-leaf parsley, 2 cups 4% cottage cheese (preferably small-curd; 16oz), ½ cup plus 2 tablespoons mayonnaise, 1 teaspoon fresh lemon juice, or to taste, 1 teaspoon of salt, ½ teaspoon black pepper

Cut cabbage into 2-inch wedges & core, then very thinly slice crosswise. Transfer to a large bowl. Add remaining ingredients & toss to coat. Let stand 15 minutes (chill up to 2 hours) to all flavors to meld

Pink Flower

Oh so beautiful is the appearance of a pink flower,
enjoy the sight of what the world has to offer us.
God's true gift has put love and joy in our hearts.
Just as the Sweetbrier you have sweet fragrance.

The Field Milkwort consist of a unique purple pink,
so pleasing I cannot take my eye off its magical colors.
A flower with two large sepals as angel wings,
Love Angel that takes us to a different world.

At times you are that wild flower of the Geranium,
bringing joy and excitement to all those around.
We run around and play building up life's gratification;
hot, wet & sticky what a way to have it a part of life.

You have beautiful legs appear like stems of an orchid,
times with silky smooth hairs that resemble Pogonia.
Very attractive flower drawing so many near you;
you a lady of character and honor offer service to one.

You are like a Pink Chameleon,
ever changing these pink flowers.
Above all you are the Pink Rose...
Depicting: Love, Gratitude, Appreciation and Elegance

Section 3

(Main Course or Entrée)

Action

Because of the action of some evil cops;
Lives of black men are being lost unjustly.
Understand the cause of an unwanted reaction.
Streets are ours black lives is not closing shop.
Help! If you took action to our cry this would not be.

We matter we've taken action on knees and marches.
Ignited the flames with your actions of death;
Nothing is what your leadership does.
Everyone must take the appropriate action;
Test yourself do onto others as you wish them on you.

Actions speak louder than words!
So make sure we are doing more,
Than what coming out our mouths.

Behind Closed Door

Amazing our love meant to soar,
In your arms I truly adore.
Oh you are so fine,
our love is so divine.
This behind,
a closed door.

Best Is Yet To Come

Better for you to be always give your best;
Loving through true grace of your heart.
Ultimate is the favor you'll be truly bless.
Speak up even give a voice to those in need;
Honor the Lord in faith you'll live in zest.

We understand God will meet our needs.
Ignite the seed of giving within us;
Never end; the best is yet to come.
Everlasting will be our faith proceeds!

Absolute Seared Scallops

Ingredients:

3 tablespoons all-purpose flour
½ teaspoon marjoram
1 tablespoon olive oil

½ teaspoon salt
½ cup dry white wine
1 tablespoon balsamic vinegar

1 ½ pounds sea scallops

Directions: Combine flour, salt & marjoram in a large zip-lock plastic bag. Add scallops, then seal & shake to coat.

Heat oil in a large non-stick skillet over medium high heat; add scallops, cook until done on each side. (about 3 to 4 minutes) Remove from pan & keep warm.

Add Wine & vinegar to pan cook 3 minutes stirring with whisk. Add scallops then remove from heat.

Serve warm.

Blacangelo

Blacangelo was not understood by others.
Lengthy intellect and skills capable of much;
Unstoppable is Sam in life he has his druthers.
Success is at hand yes his touch is really gold.
He was moving up had class envy of all mothers.

We loved his ride yet love Blacangelo even more!
In style was the king to be because he was gifted.
None like him he had swagger there are no limits.
Everyone love being with him there's was no bore.

Black Diamond

Black girl styling in her bell-bottoms,
Living the pressures of the seventies.
Understanding the Lord leads the way.
She develops & learns under these pressures;
Harden & matures she's known as the Black Diamond

World traveled Black Diamond is known to all.
Intelligent character gives her an extra shine;
None other like this gem cannot be broken.
Evolve from her surrounding and strong beliefs.

Chicken Soup

Started with an high fever,
having extreme hot flashes,
broke out into cold sweats.

Excessive pain felt in my chest,
lungs tighten, difficulty breathing.
Symptoms of a cold or heartache?

Often had a very stuffy nose,
along with watery tired eyes;
Might have come from the crying.

Dark clouds followed wherever I went,
this darkness led to a loss of appetite,
upon me fell muscle aches and exhaustion.

You arrived in my life as a ray of sunshine,
Your eyes apples for my heart bringing joy.
Washing my hands of pass heartaches.

My pain might have been common,
felt by many others before me.
Yet your love is something unique!

Touch of your hand brings hot flashes;
my heart now skips a beat of joy,
Your Love is Chicken Soup for My Soul.

Control

Beware evil lurking in your shadows;
Lying to you to control your life.
The spirit us God gave is not timid;
It gives us power, love and control.
Knowing the word we will grow.

We honor Christ who for died for sin;
It's the love of Christ that controls us.
Never fear God will be with the righteous;
control over evil is for Jesus children.
So continue to walk in faith with a grin.

Doing It Well

Been watching his great art for years;
Love his story telling on the screen.
Understanding love, hate giving cheers!
Silver screen golden he's doing it well.
His style was questioned by his peers.

We brothers and sisters got to have it
In demand for the message he brings
No in Spike there will never be no quit
Everyone is happy he got it the right way.

Down Any Road

Since a kid you've been great teacher;
learned more than I could have imagine.
Greatness of happiness I now know.

Turned me and siblings loose long ago,
yet we stayed in heart never to leave.
Follow her down any road she travels.

A diligent teacher of faith and love
committed to the word and one another.
My mother we are with you always.

Evening's Gold

As I stand there looking out the picture window,
I marvel as the evening's gold settles on the horizon.
The warmth and beauty are leaving me for the day,
I close my eyes and make a wish for it all to return.

Solar riches sink into my night's depression,
the light and nourishment disappear from the day,
that shining light that is needed to guide a lost soul,
God's nourishment that mends a now broken heart.

A great trepidation covers me like the dark of night,
It should be a time for togetherness and sharing,
yet I'm left with a rejected heart and vacated soul,
searching and praying for the one to complete me.

I prepare a dinner of Jamaican steak and shrimp,
serve with an island drink to add flare to my life,
set the table for two with the finest plates,
share this in candle light with an empty plate and chair.

Fall into bed on an oversize pillow tired from my sorrows,
a time when my mind in the weakest; I then cry the most.
I cover totally in my comforter like a turtle in its shell,
with tears streaming down my cheeks I then prayed.

Jamaican Steak & Shrimp

Ingredients

4 (8 ounce size) petite sirloin steaks
1 pound peeled and deveined raw shrimp
1 cup pineapple juice
1/3 cup soy sauce
4 teaspoons powdered ginger
Jamaican jerk seasoning
1/2 red bell pepper
1/2 green bell pepper
olive oil
pineapple chunks

Directions

Marinate steaks and shrimp overnight in marinade mixture (pineapple juice, soy sauce and ginger), turning occasionally.

Prepare grill or oven broiler. Remove meat and shrimp from marinade and cook to desired doneness. Discard marinade.

Meanwhile, stir fry the bell peppers until crisp tender with olive oil. Add pineapple and heat through.

Add jerk seasoning to meat and shrimp during final minutes of cooking. Garnish with vegetable mixture.

Serve over white, fried or yellow (for the gold effect) rice.

Everybody Loves Bacon

Been called pigs since the 70's by some;
Loathed when they abuse the innocent.
Upheld when putting away the hated scum.
Sanctified for the dangers they face daily.
Heroes they truly are...Yes everybody bacon!

We portray them as kids for images on t.v.
Insult them when we are push and abuse;
No things are not always equal between us.
Everybody loves bacon; they die it's the blues.

Scallop Chowder w/ Bacon

Ingredients:
4 bacon slices, chopped (Applewood Peppered Thick)
1 cup chopped onions   *2 cups whole milk*
1 tablespoon all-purpose flour   *½ teaspoon salt*
¼ teaspoon black pepper   *1 pound sea scallops*
1 (10-oz) package frozen mixed veggies
1 large boiling potato (peeled & cut into ¼ inch pieces
¼ teaspoon dried thyme
1/8 to ¼ cup parmesan cheese (if desired)

Directions: Cook chopped bacon in a 2-quart heavy saucepan over medium high heat, stirring occasionally, until crisp. Transfer with slotted spoon to paper towel to drain.

Add onions, potatoes to bacon fat in pan & cook about 1 minute, then sprinkle in flour & cook, stirring 1 minute. Slowly whisk in milk & bring to a boil whisking very often. Add veggies, thyme, salt & pepper & simmer, uncovered stirring occasionally, about 3 minutes.

Cut scallops in half & add to soup, then simmer just until scallops are cooked through, about 5 minutes. Sprinkle with bacon.

Add parmesan cheese to bowls for garnish & add flavor if desired.

Sea Scallops can be subsisted for 2 8 oz. cans of baby clams only drain one if in clam juice.

Gorilla Glue

Bonded by this ambassador that spoke bold.
Lady of God and love she's a great being!
United by her character has a heart of gold.
Strong family values held like gorilla glue.
Her wording upheld you did what you told.

We honor the ambassador of God she's the glue.
In our hearts forever much love carried;
Never to forget as we pray we give thanks above.
Everlasting praise we sing those bonded in her crew

Ephesians 6:20

House Call

When the telephone starts to ring.
You wander is that Trump on the other end?
If it is there's no good to come of the call,
not as comic as speaking by the pale moon light.

Man seems to be pure evil walking with us.
It's supposed to be a government for the people;
he does not put himself behind the desk
instead he is out front for all to see who he is.

He has a beautiful house for many to see;
Yet no one wants to see him in it.
So when he makes that grand house call
no one accepts his invite they rip up the card.

So when the telephone starts to ring again
You check the caller id then pick it up now.
Then say "Sorry Mr. Trump I'm busy"
Letting him know you stand for something.

Lessons Won

Years passed...
We refuse to lose,
precious lessons
are to be won.

Evil tries to wash
over us; we remain
focus on the light.

Faith is now
our habit of life
to forever more walk.

At last habit cast
as a stone that
builds a divine bridge
to our precious Lord.

Leverage

Bargaining chip you make me out to be;
Leverage you never have over me.
Under the word of God how I live my life.
Sin no factor since Jesus shed His blood
You better check your ego at the door.

Walking in faith I became a strong lady;
Independent! God has all the authority now.
No one will ever claim leverage in my life.
So I say choose wisely when speaking to me.

Like Ali

Boy you're getting in my space;
Like Ali I'll sting you like a bee.
Understand I'll put you in place.
Shh! Shut your mouth right now;
Hurry up back up out my face.

Were tight called ourselves family.
I'll be on you like a swarm of bees.
Never letting up with the one, two.
Encourage I'll handle things with ease.

Promise Keeper

Be a person of bono fide word;
Let what you say be who you are.
Understanding promise is kept by the Lord;
Sending you the Holy Spirit as a friend.
Heaven is promise if you take the word in accord.

We shall make promise to follow Him above
Ignite the seed that is deep in us all.
Never sinning always walking in faith;
Everlasting life our promise of everlasting love.

Remaining Gem

Been a rich loving family legacy;
Much pride in this blood and name.
She was born from a large clan;
When she was born they said she
Was more precious than jewels.

She then got the name of Ba Ba.
Powerful family all have great worth;
All are miss she's the remaining gem.
She's gone from Ba Ba to Black Diamond.
Nothing going to compare to her.

She Needn't Be

But it takes time to mend a heart
Love at first brought you together;
Understand now it's time to part.
She needn't be in your life anymore.
Heartbroken she's not your sweetheart.

Weeks and weeks you'll a change person.
Inner soul search you're at peace.
No demons; she needn't be bye bye!
Everyone saw your life with her worsen.

When The Smoke Clears

There was much terror when the thunder
came one roar right after the other one.
Bodies were shaken; many fell to the ground;
pain and fear came like it never did before.

Smoke soon filled the air of a beautiful day;
within it screams, confusion covered with blood.
Looking for your love one amidst the chaos,
questions of why and will everyone be alright.

We are just flesh and bone left scattered around;
yet I know when the smoke clears we'll be more.
With confidence we'll stand up and proclaim...
"I will not fear what man has and will continue to do!"

The Lord has brought us through many times before.
So when the smoke clears from my mind,
I will say a prayer for those hurt and their families.
Give thanks to God and those that ran into the smoke.

Blessing to so many and keep running!
Hebrews 13:6

Peach-Glazed Barbecued Pork Chops & Peaches

Ingredients: 3 cups chopped peaches (about 1 ½ pounds)

1 cup dry white wine	1 teaspoon truffle salt-divided
¼ cup sugar	¼ teaspoon smoked black pepper-divided
1/8 cup of truffle oil	
2 tablespoons molasses	1 teaspoon Chile power
½ teaspoon paprika	¼ teaspoon ground red pepper
6 (6 oz.) bone-in pork chops	6 peaches, halved, pitted

(pork chops about ½ inch thick; glaze works well on chicken also)

Directions: Combine peaches, wine & sugar in a small saucepan; bring to a boil. Cover, reduce heat & simmer 25 minutes. Uncover & simmer 5 more minutes.

Place peach mixture in a food processor; process until smooth. Add ¾ teaspoon of salt, 1/8 teaspoon of black pepper, vinegar, molasses, chile power, truffle oil, paprika & red pepper, pulse to combine. Let stand 5 minutes.

Place half of the peach mixture in a large heavy-duty plastic zip lock bag. Save the other half for basting. Add pork chops to bag seal bag & refrigerate for 30 minutes to 4 hours

Preheat grill. Remove chops from bag & toss marinade. Sprinkle pork chops with remaining ¼ teaspoon salt & remaining 1/8 teaspoon black pepper.

Place pork chops & peach halves on grill rack coated with cooking spray 7 grill until done. (about 10 minutes) Baste with remaining mixture every 2-3 minutes. Turning once. When finish enjoy.

Whimpering Miracle

Sets out as he does everyday
the constant work he is assigned.
Whimpered cries in a distance,
first thought to be dying animal.

The cries grow drawing him near.
It is the whimpering of the baby,
maybe Gods' attention to his child.
All that is certain time for a miracle.

In a bin of unwanted food and boxes,
there's a bag outlined with new life.
Baby's wrapped in a shirt for comfort,
ushered to a chest to discover a heartbeat.

The warmth, comfort and miracle of God
transferred in care of a workingman.
Once a mother's unwanted trash;
Now a treasure of this world and God

Your Breath

Your Breath...
Is sweet harmonize life,
Brings love & jazz to all.

It's a simple breeze,
As you walk by,
Kisses my face.

Your Breath...
So soft & subtle,
As you whisper I love you.

It's a strong gale wind,
The moment you said I do.
Knocked me to my knees.

Your Breath...
Very strong & intoxicating,
When I slipped under its spell.

It's a smooth calm wind,
When you say lay with me,
Makes my heart skip a beat.

Your Breath is the love inside my heart.

Section 4

(Chef's Special)

Cry For You

You said you were touched in places,
that no adult should ever touch a kid.
Because of these actions,
I cry for you now!

I'm sorry that you were scared,
no child should live with hatred and fear!
Do not anger at yourself, you did nothing wrong.
Fear not the person who claims love for you.

No need to worry,
your soul is pure.
They face eternal damnation!
For that I cheer for you!

I can't take back what has happened,
sorry I can't take away the pain.
You do not have to cry anymore.
I will cry for you.

Since I could not help,
I WILL CRY FOR YOU!

Demons

Evil living among us,
walking & smiling trying to befriend.
Wearing mask, fooling everyone.

If this is love "why?"
Do I hurt so much,
Feel so dirty?

I want to scream,
"Please stop doing this
I do not like it!"

I want to tell someone, "but who?"
Will they hurt me also?
They claim to love me too...

There are no monsters in the closet,
None hiding under the bed.
They sit at the Thanksgiving table.

Hugging me longer than most.
Smiling at me with evil eyes,
Touching me in places I do not like.

Yes, this will be stopped!
Time to make a stand...
Their Demons will be exorcised!

Not because of my love for them,
Because I love myself.
I am special. I am somebody!

Author's Comments This is for those who have endured pain and evil that most of us never thought could exist. I Love You All!! For your pain. I still "Cry For You" For those new to my work this is a follow up to "Cry For You"

Demon's Cry

Sun setting in the distance along the coast,
beautiful rainbow hews of violet red and blue.
Calmness of the moment does not fill you,
you are consumed with sadness and grief.

Sun setting brings the darkness of the night.
The night is for the demons that haunt you,
demons that preyed on your sweet innocence.
You lie there and cry hoping for the best.

The tears do not flow down your face,
it is your heart that cries out for you.
Lay there eyes close and shaking with fear,
your pity no one hears and comes to comfort.

This evil robbed you of a happy childhood,
brought you down into the depths of hell.
Seen and feared things no human should encountered,
all of this from the early stages of life.

I look into your beautiful eyes!
I see the pain inside of your heart,
you try to hide it and bury it deep.
It's my weight to bear now

I open my heart to fill you with love,
exorcize these demons from your life.
I embrace you in God's comfort and love.
You need not to cry anymore.

I shall cry for you.

Monster Bash

You think back to that magical day,
That ill-fated day you said "I Do".
Across you stood a monster in a tuxedo.

In that glorious house of the Lord,
He vowed to love, honor and protect you,
In front of 75 people and God.

He swore that no evil would come between you,
This touched you, and a tear crossed your cheek,
You locked those beautiful words in your heart.

Now the monster is out of the closet,
Your body quakes when he's angry,
All the monster wants to do is bash.

The first time should have been the last,
Your things in a suitcase, then out the door,
Yes, he cried with you "I'll never do it again".

Your kind heart overflowed with forgiveness,
This was the invitation he so needed,
Enabling this monster to do as he pleases.

You want to cry out to someone,
That would listen, and would understand.
You feel so stupid and ashamed!

To him the ring on his finger means,
He has the right to rape and beat you,
Because he thinks you belong to him.

He no longer rapes you,
You give the monster what he wants,
You lie there listening to his grunts and cry.

You either bow to him now,
Or take his terrible beatings,
He gets what he wants anyway.

This does not stop all the bashing,
The monster needs to be in control.
You just pray this is the day you die!

When the doctor enquired.
"Mrs. Smith how did you break your arm?"
A tear in your eye you said "I fell down the stairs".

You put on all the fancy makeup,
Wear your nice designer long sleeves,
That won't hide the scars of a broken heart.

Meatloaf, Old School Italian Style

Ingredients:

- *2/3 cup torn crust-less day-old Italian bread*
- *1/3 cup milk*
- *1 lb ground beef*
- *2 lg eggs, lighten beaten*
- *1 teaspoon salt*
- ¼ teaspoon black pepper
- ¼ lb baked ham, finely chopped (1 cup)
- *2 oz. sliced provolone, finely chopped (1/2 cup)*
- ¼ cup fine dry bread *crumbs (not seasoned)*
- *3 hard-boiled large eggs, peeled*

- ➤ *Directions: Put oven rack in middle position & preheat oven to 350*F. Oil a 9 inch square baking pan.*
- ➤ *Stir together bread & milk in a large bowl & let stand 10 minutes*
- ➤ *Add beef, lightly beaten eggs, salt & pepper to bread mixture & mix with your hands until combined, then mix in ham & cheese.*
- ➤ *Scatter 2 tablespoons of breadcrumbs into a 8 x 4 inch loaf pan Spread half the meat mixture into loaf pan over the bread crumbs, then arrange the hard boiled eggs about ½ inch apart in a row down the middle of the meat mixture. Cover eggs with remaining of the meat mixture. Then sprinkle the remaining breadcrumbs over the top*

Bake until thermometer inserted near center of loaf (but avoiding egg) registers 155*F, 50-60 minutes. Let stand

Warm Lentil Salad With Smoked Sausage

Ingredients

- 2 cups fresh lentils (about 10 oz.) picked over & rinsed
- 1 Bay leaf
- 6 cups of water
- 3 teaspoon of finely chopped garlic
- ¼ teaspoon black pepper
- 1 medium onion, finely chopped (1cup)
- 2 carrots, cut and dice
- 2 celery ribs cut and dice
- ¾ pound smoked sausage, cut into ¼ inch slices
- ¼ cup red-wine vinegar
- 1 tablespoon Dijon mustard
- ½ teaspoon dried thyme crumbled
- 1 teaspoon salt
- ½ cup plus 2tablespoons extra-virgin olive oil
- 1/4 cup chopped fresh flat-leaf parsley
- 1/4 cup finely chopped scallions (3 to 4 scallions)

Directions: Bring lentils, water & bay leaf to a boil in a 2 to 3 quart heavy saucepan, then reduce heat & simmer , covered, until almost tender, about 15 minutes. Stir in ½ teaspoon salt, then simmer lentils, cover, until tender but not falling apart, about 3 to 5 minutes. While lentils simmer cook onion, carrots, celery, garlic, thyme, ¼ teaspoon salt & 1/8 teaspoon pepper in 2 tablespoon oil in heavy skillet over moderately low heat, stirring occasionally, until vegetables are just softened, 7 to 9 minutes.

Make vinaigrette by whisking together vinegar, mustard & remaining ¼ salt & 1/8 pepper in a bowl. Add remaining ½ cup oil in a slow stream, whisking until blended well.

Drain lentils in a colander, discarding bay leaf & return to sauce pan along with vegetable mixture & vinaigrette. Cook over low heat, stirring until heated through. Keep warm, covered.

Brown smoked sausage in clean skillet browning evenly on each side stir sausage with parsley into lentils & enjoy!

Section 5

(Beverages)

California Eve

Secluded spot on a California beach.
A cool brisk breeze blows off the water.
I settle onto the blanket with my lady.

Admiring the beautiful orange of the sun,
I pull you closer to smell your sweetness.
Talked of the comfort we brought each other.

Sun sets bringing more coolness to the night.
Our lips come together; you taste of berry wine.
As the breeze hits us I'm crunching in expectation.

Coffee Break

Here I sit with Little Miss Coffee.
Valuing the time we spend together,
Togetherness with you is to be treasured.

I reach out to clasp your soft hand,
Looking into your sweet seductive eyes.
From my heart with love I say "Thank You!"

Knowing you has awakened my mind,
Brought loving warmth to my body,
Above all you have comforted my soul.

Never Bitter Always Strong!

Hocus Pocus

Most would say "Abracadabra,"
your magic word was a simple "Hello,"
I was taken in by your beauty,
Then followed that super fine body.

Thought you gave me the evil eye,
something much more than a twinkle,
your lovely browns left me with a mysterious feeling.
Some sort of trance...Something shall we say hypnotic?

I'm very much bewitch by you my lady,
so fascinated by everything you do.
You're Luscious! The good witch of my soul.
Every good thing I've done is because of you.

Alakazam...One great big flash of light,
you've now created something out of nothing,
I once had an empty desolate heart,
it was then filled with unexplained joy.

You gave me what I thought to be smooth drinks,
I sipped on Patron Mango freeze & Pineapple Martinis.
Ohhh...It was something stronger than that,
your sweet magic potions sliding down my throat.

I downed a glass of Alize Rose,
then floated away on your gentle trade wind.
Hocus Pocus...Just like magic, I'm in love!

Just Like You

When you see the man on the corner,
What do you see?
Along with your coffee change,
You give him your sorrow and pity.

He does not want your sorrow,
Needs no one to feel sorry for him.
He does not need your pity;
There's nothing pitiful about him.

What he deserves is your respect,
People used to see him as they see you,
Once he was thought of as a man just like you,
The man on the corner.

Once had the gifts of success,
Which you tend to take for granted,
He once had your respect.
Cherish your life and what you have.

He too had the fancy car, big house, and nice job.
By some strange twist of life, he lost it all,
The same unfortunate fate could await you,
When you see him on the corner.

Give him not your coffee change;
Offer him your respect.
Once he was thought of as a man.
JUST LIKE YOU!

Oversize Cappuccino

Here I sit with bible
on dawn of a new day.

It shall be my cappuccino
first intake of the Lord's Day.

Oversize cappuccino in hand
the mind awakens from slumber.

Now clothe in the armor of Light
I'll gratify the Lord not the flesh.

Bringing God's radiant
glory to another day.

Romans 13: 11-14

Special Child

Be amaze she had a special child!
Lovely gift from God is my sister,
Understand she brings a big smile!
She's like a Guadalajara punch better aged.
Honored as a child she was a bit wild!

We love her dearly our sibling leader.
Intoxicating kiss like that sweet punch;
Never enough for her loving husband.
Everyone celebrates the special child!

Guadalajara Punch

- *Ingredients:* 1 fresh pineapple, cut into bite-sized chunks
- 1 liter bottle tequila Blanco
- 2 cups tequila reposado
- 1/2 cup fresh lime juice
- 6 cups fresh orange juice
- 46 ounces unsweetened pineapple juice
- 4 oranges, cut into bite-sized wedges
- 1/2 medium watermelon, cut into bite-sized chunks or triangles with peel,
- 3 lemons, sliced, 6 limes, quartered,
- 3 small ruby grapefruit, cut in bite-sized wedges,
- 2 star fruit sliced into star shapes, 4 cans (12 ounces each) Squirt soda

Directions

Place pineapple chunks in a wide-mouthed glass jar. Add tequilas, juices, and sliced oranges. Chill overnight. Add watermelon, lemons, limes, grapefruit, and star fruit and chill several more hours, stirring occasionally. Add Squirt immediately before serving

Chef's notes: Flavor of punch improves with age best to prepare 24 hours before event. It keeps for day in fridge yet lemon, limes & grapefruit will become bitter. So best to have a large crowd to serve to. They will enjoy. Great outdoor grill drink.

Tip Toe

It's now the big party night
what everyone been waiting for.
You and I have made eye contact
circle the room to find each other.

Stand there with drinks in hand;
talking about happens in our life.
Many would call it small talk
yet it is humongous for you & I.

Party is now coming to a close
a few has had too much to drink.
My knees wobble I take a stumble
I'm sure it's not the wine it's you.

Put others up in the bedrooms;
lay me down gently on the couch.
Time pass I'm sure everyone is sleep;
I then tip toe down the hallway.

So careful as not to disturb nobody,
my business with you is our concern.
Knock so gently on your bedroom door
Greeted with an alluring smile and kiss.

Section 6

(Desserts)

Chocolate Pecan Pie

My dear lady you are like a chocolate pecan pie,
the perfect complement to any meal.
A delightful pleasure to behold.

It starts with your perfect round face,
Just like an impeccable 9 in. round pie,
A flawless creation invaluable work of art!

Just as a slice is a great hold in my hand,
you are distinguished hold for any man.
Many are seeking this fine treasure of God.

Your intelligence like the nuts of this pie,
plentiful and enjoyable never too much.
No matter warm or cool you are always wanted.

Your love like this pie cuts into perfect slices,
an elation to us all whom it's shared with.
Your heart warm and giving of its greatness.

Skin is like the finest chocolate,
so creamy and rich with great texture.
Lastly your lips are sweet, *blissful and idealistic.*

Yes you my dear lady are...
Chocolate Pecan Pie!

Dessert

If life is a meal,
your Love is the perfect compliment.
Such a fine sweet dessert!

After a hard day's work,
dealing with life's chaos,
it's pleasing to come home to you.

Just as mom's apple pie,
the scent of you,
brings a smile to my face.

Sometimes I wonder,
why can't I skip the meal?
Go straight to dessert.

I thought there was nothing finer,
than chocolate ganache cheesecake,
until you held me in your arms.

Your sweet, sweet love,
is like peach clobber,
very warm and inviting.

You're my life... Just Dessert.

Dewberry Dumping

It's a high Texas summer heat
kids do not feel it they're having fun.
Running around with bucket bumping
into one another picking Texas dewberries

Mom knew the spots where to go for them;
it's amazing she always does the berry hound.
Kids are sneaking a few every now and then
plump and juicy they just couldn't resist them.

Back to grandma's house sweat on their brow
give her the buckets full of those juicy berries.
She rinse them off then slow brew on stovetop
dropping homemade butter and sugar in them.

Ice Cream

The Lord's word like premium ice cream;
so rich and fulfilling to all who take it in.
Always coming back for more to be satisfied.

Cooling a hot evil devil tormented soul;
forever soothing to a shattered lonely heart.
Touching all verities of life and culture

No matter your season of life it's welcome.
Whatever you'll going through it refreshes
You scream, I scream, we all will scream...

For the Ice Cream of our Lord.

Juice and Cookies

Enticed in with your rhythmic hips,
love the sweet neater of your lips.
Top line such a high class treat,
league of your own you are elite.
Lovemaking you're no rookie,
you are my juice and cookies

Marbled Lemon Curd Cheesecake

Ingredients: For Lemon Curd...
1 teaspoon finely grated fresh lemon zest   ½ cup lemon juice
½ cup sugar   3 large eggs   ½ stick unsalted butter cut in
small pieces
For Crust...
1 1/3 cups finely ground graham cracker crumbs
1/3 cup sugar   1/8 teaspoon salt
5 tablespoons unsalted butter (melted)
For Filling...
3 (8 oz.) packages cream cheese, (softened)
1 cup sugar   3 large eggs
¾ cup sour cream   1 teaspoon pure vanilla extract

Special Equipment: 9 to 9 ½ inch spring form pan for pie crust.

Make Lemon Curd: Whisk together lemon zest, lemon juice, sugar & eggs in a heavy saucepan. Add butter & cook over low heat, whisking often, until curd is thick enough to hold whisk marks & first bubbles appear on surface about 7 minutes.

Make & Bake Crust: Put oven rack in middle position & preheat oven to 350*F. Invert bottom of spring form pan then lock on side. Stir together crust ingredients in bowl, then press onto & up 1 inch side of spring form pan. Place spring form pan in a shallow baking pan & bake 10 minutes. Then cool crust totally in spring form on a rack.

Make Filling & Bake Cheesecake: Reduce oven temperature to 300*F.

Beat together cream cheese & sugar in a bowl with an electric mixer at medium speed until smooth, 1 to 2 minutes. Reduce speed to low & add eggs 1 at a time, beating until well blended. Beat in sour cream & vanilla until combined. Pour two thirds of cream cheese filling into crust, then spoon half of lemon curd over filling & swirl curd into filling with small knife. Repeat with remaining filling & curd.

Bake cheesecake until set 1 ½ from edge but center trembles about 45 minutes. Transfer spring form to a rack; & & run knife around edge to loosen. Cool completely about 2 hours then chill uncovered at least 4 hours. Remove side of spring form before serving.

www.ingramcontent.com/pod-product-compliance
Lightning Source LLC
Chambersburg PA
CBHW020325130626
46549CB00003B/1025